P9-CJY-845

THE WONDERS OF THE HOLY NAME

BOOKS BY
FATHER PAUL O'SULLIVAN, O.P.

THE WONDERS OF THE HOLY NAME

by
Father Paul O'Sullivan, O.P.
(E.D.M.)

"For which cause God also hath exalted him, and hath given him a name which is above all names: That in the name of Jesus every knee should bow, of those that are in heaven, on earth, and under the earth." —Philippians 2:9–10

TAN Books
An Imprint of Saint Benedict Press, LLC
Charlotte, North Carolina

APPROVED BY HIS EMINENCE
THE CARDINAL PATRIARCH OF LISBON
March 4, 1947

First published circa 1946 by the former Edições do Corpo Santo, Lisbon, Portugal. Retypeset and republished in 1993 by TAN Books, an Imprint of Saint Benedict Press, LLC, with permission of Saint Martin de Porres Apostolate, Dublin, Ireland.

The type in this book is the property of TAN Books, and may not be reproduced, in whole or in part, without written permission from the Publisher.

ISBN: 978-0-89555-490-1

Library of Congress Catalog Card No.: 93-60345

Printed and bound in the United States of America.

TAN Books
An Imprint of Saint Benedict Press, LLC
Charlotte, North Carolina
2012

*This booklet is lovingly dedicated
to the Sweet Mother of Jesus.
No one loves the name of Jesus
as she does.*

LETTERS OF APPROBATION

The Wonders of the Holy Name has received the warmest approval of many Archbishops and Bishops. We quote two of these:

CARDINAL'S PALACE, LISBON
March 4, 1947

I approve and recommend with all my heart the little book entitled "The Wonders of the Holy Name."

+ M. , Cardinal Patriarca

March 7, 1947

My Dear Father Paul O'Sullivan,

My cordial thanks for the kind offer of your beautiful book, *The Wonders of the Holy Name*, which I have read with much interest. I see that it explains with great clearness and precision the doctrine of the Holy Name, a doctrine so dear to the Church.

Certainly the perusal of this book will enkindle in the hearts of its readers a boundless confidence in the Omnipotence of the Holy Name.

I am, therefore, very pleased to approve warmly this latest work of yours, which is a worthy link in the long chain of your zealous and useful publications.

Blessing you with all my heart, I remain with the highest esteem,

Yours very sincerely,
✝ PETER CIRIACI, Archbishop of Tarsus
Apostolic Nuncio

LETTER FROM THE MASTER GENERAL
OF THE DOMINICAN ORDER

SANTA SABINA

August 29, 1945

To the Reverend Father Paul H. O'Sullivan

Reverend Dear Father:

We are aware of how you have dedicated yourself for the past fifty years to all kinds of Catholic Propaganda, especially the Propaganda of the Press.

Your activity has been indeed marvelous. Now you have launched a veritable crusade in favor of the Holy Name of Jesus, a crusade which has been crowned with very great success.

All this fills our heart with joy, and therefore we send you our paternal blessing and the blessing of our Holy Father St, Dominic.

We beg you to accept the assurance of our sincere affection.

Fr. M. S. Gillet, O.P.
Master General

Contents

To the Reader

Dear Friend,

Read this booklet slowly and with attention, not once, but many times, and you will thank God all the rest of your life.

It will give you much happiness, and it will enable you to obtain from God wonderful graces and blessings.

It teaches the wonders of the Holy Name of Jesus, which few Christians understand.

The frequent repetition of this divine name will save you from much suffering and great dangers.

The world is now threatened with the direst calamities. Each one of us can do much to save himself from the impending evils, and we can do much to help the world, the Church and our Holy Father the Pope, simply by repeating frequently, "*Jesus, Jesus, Jesus*." (See page 3).

—The Author

THE WONDERS OF
THE HOLY NAME

Chapter 1

The Wonders of the Holy Name

We have been hearing and have been repeating from childhood the Holy Name of Jesus, but alas, many, very many, have no adequate idea of the great wonders of this Holy Name!

What do you know, Dear Reader, about the Name of Jesus? You know that it is a holy name and that you must bow your head reverently when you say it. That is very little. It is as if you looked at a closed book and merely glanced at the title on the cover. You know nothing of all the beautiful thoughts in the book itself.

Even so, when you pronounce the Name of Jesus you know very little of the treasures hidden in it.

This Divine Name is in truth a mine of riches; it is the fount of the highest holiness and the secret of the greatest happiness that a man can hope to enjoy on this earth. Read and see.

It is so powerful, so certain, that it never fails to produce in our souls the most wonderful results. It consoles the saddest heart and makes the weakest sinner strong. It obtains for us all kinds of favors

1

and graces, spiritual and temporal.

Two things we must do. First of all, we must understand clearly the meaning and value of the Name of Jesus.

Secondly, we must get into the habit of saying it devoutly, frequently, hundreds and hundreds of times every day. Far from being a burden, it will be an immense joy and consolation.

Chapter 2

What Does the Name of Jesus Mean?

The Holy Name of Jesus is, first of all, an all-powerful prayer. Our Lord Himself solemnly promises that whatever we ask the Father in His Name we shall receive. God never fails to keep His word.

When, therefore, we say, "Jesus," let us ask God for all we need with absolute confidence of being heard.

For this reason, the Church ends her prayer with the words "through Jesus Christ," which gives the prayer a new and divine efficacy.

But the Holy Name is something still greater.

Each time we say, "Jesus," we give God infinite joy and glory, for we offer Him all the infinite merits of the Passion and Death of Jesus Christ.

St. Paul tells us that Jesus merited the Name *Jesus* by His Passion and Death.

Each time we say, "Jesus," let us clearly wish to offer God all the Masses being said all over the world for all our intentions. We thus share in these thousands of Masses.

Each time we say, "Jesus," we gain 300 days indulgence,* which we may apply to the souls in Purgatory, thus relieving and liberating very many of these holy souls from their awful pains. They thus become our best friends and pray for us with incredible fervor.

Each time we say, "Jesus," it is an act of perfect love, for we offer to God the infinite love of Jesus.

The Holy Name of Jesus saves us from innumerable evils and delivers us especially from the power of the devil, who is constantly seeking to do us harm.

The Name of Jesus gradually fills our souls with a peace and a joy we never had before.

The Name of Jesus gives us such strength that our sufferings become light and easy to bear.

---

*Although the Church's regulations on Indulgences, including those regarding ejaculations, have changed, perhaps we may still hope to obtain these same Indulgences from God if we ask Him for them with great confidence. —*Editor*, 1993.

What Must We Do?

St. Paul tells us that we must do all we do, whether in word or work, in the Name of Jesus. "All whatsoever you do in word or in work, do all in the name of the Lord Jesus Christ . . ." (*Col.* 3:17).

In this way, every act becomes an act of love and of merit, and, moreover, we receive grace and help to do all our actions perfectly and well.

We must therefore do our best to form the habit of saying, "Jesus, Jesus, Jesus," very often every day. We can do so when dressing, when working—no matter what we are doing—when walking, in moments of sadness, at home and in the street, everywhere.

Nothing is easier if only we do it methodically. We can say it countless times every day.

Bear in mind that each time we say, "Jesus," devoutly, 1) we give God great glory, 2) we receive great graces for ourselves, 3) and we help the souls in Purgatory.

We shall now quote a few examples to show the power of the Holy Name.

Chapter 3

The World in Danger
Saved by the Holy Name

In the year 1274 great evils threatened the world. The Church was assailed by fierce enemies from within and without. So great was the danger that the **Pope, Gregory X,** who then reigned, called a council of Bishops in Lyons to determine on the best means of saving society from the ruin that menaced it. Among the many means proposed, the Pope and Bishops chose what they considered the easiest and most efficacious of all, viz., the frequent repetition of the Holy Name of Jesus.

The Holy Father then begged the Bishops of the world and their priests to call on the Name of Jesus and to urge their peoples to place all their confidence in this all-powerful Name, repeating it constantly with boundless trust. The Pope entrusted the Dominicans especially with the glorious task of preaching the wonders of the Holy Name in every country, a work they accomplished with unbounded zeal.

Their Franciscan brothers ably seconded them. St. Bernardine of Siena and St. Leonard of Port-

Maurice were ardent apostles of the Name of Jesus.

Their efforts were crowned with success so that the enemies of the Church were overthrown, the dangers that threatened society disappeared and peace once more reigned supreme.

This is a most important lesson for us because, in these our own days, dreadful sufferings are crushing many countries, and still greater evils threaten all the others.

No government or governments seem strong and wise enough to stem this awful torrent of evils. There is but one remedy, and that is *prayer*.

Every Christian must turn to God and ask Him to have mercy on us. The easiest of all prayers, as we have seen, is the Name of Jesus.

Everyone without exception can invoke this holy name hundreds of times a day, not only for his own intentions, but also to ask God to deliver the world from impending ruin.

It is amazing what one person who prays can do to save his country and save society. We read in Holy Scripture how **Moses** saved by his prayer the people of Israel from destruction, and how one pious woman, **Judith of Betulia,** saved her city and her people when the rulers were in despair and about to surrender themselves to their enemies.

Again, we know that the two cities of **Sodom and Gomorrha,** which God destroyed by fire for their sins and crimes, would have been pardoned had there been only ten good men to pray for them!

Over and over again we read of kings, emperors, statesmen and famous military commanders who placed all their trust in prayer, thus working wonders. If the prayers of one man can do much, what will not the prayers of many do?

The Name of Jesus is the shortest, the easiest and the most powerful of prayers. Everyone can say it, even in the midst of his daily work. God cannot refuse to hear it.

Let us then invoke the Name of Jesus, asking Him to save us from the calamities that threaten us.

Chapter 4

The Plague in Lisbon: The City Saved by the Holy Name

A devastating plague broke out in Lisbon in 1432. All who could do so fled in terror from the city and thus carried the plague to every corner of the entire country of Portugal.

Thousands of men, women and children of all classes were swept away by the cruel sickness. So virulent was the epidemic that men died everywhere, at table, in the streets, in their houses, in the shops, in the marketplaces, in the churches. To use the words of historians, it flashed like lightning from man to man, or from a coat, a hat or any garment that had been used by the plague-stricken. Priests, doctors and nurses were carried off in such numbers that the bodies of many lay unburied in the streets, so that the dogs licked up the blood and ate the flesh of the dead, becoming as a result themselves infected with the dread disease and spreading it still more widely among the unfortunate people.

Among those who assisted the dying with unflagging zeal was a venerable bishop, Monsignor André

Dias, who lived in the Convent or Monastery of St. Dominic. This holy man, seeing that the epidemic, far from diminishing, grew every day in intensity, and despairing of human help, urged the unhappy people to call on **the Holy Name of Jesus.** He was seen wherever the disease was fiercest, urging, imploring the sick and the dying, as well as those who had not as yet been stricken down, to repeat, **"Jesus, Jesus."** "Write it on cards," he said, "and keep those cards on your persons; place them at night under your pillows; place them on your doors; but above all, constantly invoke with your lips and in your hearts this most powerful Name."

He went about as an angel of peace filling the sick and the dying with courage and confidence. The poor sufferers felt within them a new life, and calling on Jesus, they wore the cards on their breasts or carried them in their pockets.

Then summoning them to the great Church of St. Dominic, he once more spoke to them of the power of **the Name of Jesus** and blessed water in the same Holy Name, ordering all the people to sprinkle themselves with it and sprinkle it on the faces of the sick and the dying. Wonder of wonders! The sick got well, the dying arose from their agonies, the plague ceased and the city was delivered in a few days from the most awful scourge that had ever visited it.

The news spread to the whole country and all began, with one accord, to call on **the Name of**

Jesus. In an incredibly short time all Portugal was freed from the dread sickness.

The grateful people, mindful of the marvels they had witnessed, continued their love and confidence in the Name of our Saviour, so that in all their troubles, in all dangers, when evils of any kind threatened them, they invoked the Name of Jesus. Confraternities were formed in the churches, processions of the Holy Name were made monthly, altars were raised in honor of this blessed name, so that the greatest curse that had ever fallen on the country was transformed into the greatest blessing.

For long centuries this great confidence in the Name of Jesus continued in Portugal and thence spread to Spain, to France, and to the whole world.

Chapter 5

Genseric the Goth

In the reign of Genseric, the Arian King of the Goths, one of the King's favorite courtiers, the Count of Armogasto, was converted from Arianism and joined the Catholic Church.

The King, on hearing of the fact, fell into a violent fury and, calling the young nobleman to his presence, tried by every means in his power to induce him to recant and return to the Arian sect. Neither threats nor promises availed. The Count refused all overtures and held fast to his new-found faith. Genseric then gave vent to his fury and ordered the young man to be bound with strong cords as tightly as the brawny executioners could draw them. The torment was intense, but the victim showed no sign of pain. He repeated two or three times, "Jesus, Jesus, Jesus," and lo, the cords snapped like spider webs and fell at his feet!

Enraged beyond measure, the tyrant now commanded that the sinews of oxen, hard and tough as wire, should be brought. The Count was again bound, and the King bade the executioners use their utmost strength. Once more their victim invoked the Name of Jesus, and the new thongs, like the old, snapped like threads. Genseric, foaming with rage, ordered the martyr to be bound by the feet and hung from the branches of a tree, head downwards.

Smiling at this new mode of torture, Count Armogasto folded his arms on his bosom and, repeating the Holy Name, fell into a tranquil sleep, as though he were lying on a soft and comfortable couch.

Chapter 6

D. Melchior Smiles at His Tormentors

We have another incident of a similar kind narrated of the Chinese Martyr, the Venerable Dominican Bishop, D. Melchior.

In one of the many persecutions which raged in China and which gave so many Saints to the Church, this holy bishop was seized and, after having undergone the most brutal torments, was condemned to a cruel death.

He was dragged to the marketplace in the midst of a howling mob, who came to gloat over his sufferings.

They stripped him of his garments, and five executioners, armed with rough-edged swords, proceeded to chop off his fingers one by one, joint by joint, then his arms, then his legs, causing him excruciating agony. Finally, they hacked the flesh from his poor body and broke his bones.

During this prolonged martyrdom, no sign of pain was visible on the Bishop's countenance. He was smiling and saying aloud, slowly, **"Jesus, Jesus, Jesus,"** which, to the amazement of his executioners, gave him this wonderful strength.

Neither cry nor groan escaped from his lips until finally, after hours of torture, he quietly breathed his last, with the same lovely smile lingering on his face.

What wonderful consolation would we too not feel, when confined to bed with sickness or racked by pain, if we repeated devoutly the Name of **Jesus.**

Many people find it hard to sleep.

They will find help and consolation by invoking in these sleepless moments the Holy Name, and very probably they will fall into a tranquil slumber.

St. Alexander and the Pagan Philosophers

During the reign of the Emperor Constantine, the Christian Religion was constantly and rapidly making progress,

In Constantinople itself the pagan philosophers felt much aggrieved at seeing many of their adepts deserting the old religion and joining the new. They pleaded with the Emperor himself, demanding that in justice they should get a hearing and be allowed to hold a public conference with the bishop of the Christians. **St. Alexander,** who at the time ruled the See of Constantinople, was a holy man, but not a keen logician.

He did not for that reason fear to meet the representative of the pagan philosophers, who was an astute dialectician and an eloquent orator. On the appointed day, before a vast assembly of learned men, the philosopher began a carefully prepared attack on the Christian teaching. The holy bishop listened for some time **and then pronounced the Name of Jesus,** which at once confounded the philosopher, who not only completely lost the thread of his discourse, but was utterly unable, even with the aid of his colleagues, to return to the attack.

St. Christiana, a young Christian girl, was a slave in Kurdistan, a region almost entirely pagan. It was the custom in that country when a child was gravely ill that the mother should take it in her arms to the houses of her friends and ask them if they knew of any remedy that might benefit or cure the little one. On one of these occasions, a mother brought her sick child to the house where Christiana lived.

On being asked if she knew of a remedy for that sickness, she looked at the child and said: **"Jesus, Jesus."**

In an instant the dying child smiled and leapt with joy. It was completely cured.

This extraordinary fact soon became known and reached the ears of the Queen, who herself was an invalid. She gave orders that Christiana should be brought to her presence,

On arriving at the palace, Christiana was asked by the royal patient if she could with the same remedy cure her own disorder, which had baffled the skill of the physicians. Once more Christiana pronounced with great confidence: **"Jesus, Jesus,"** and again this divine Name was glorified. The Queen instantly recovered her health.

A third wonder was yet to be worked. Some days after the cure of the Queen, the King found himself suddenly face to face with certain death. Escape seemed impossible. Mindful of the divine power of the Holy Name, which he had witnessed in the cure of his wife, his majesty called out, **"Jesus, Jesus,"** whereupon he was snatched from the dreadful peril. Calling in his own turn for the little slave, he learned from her the truths of Christianity, which he and a great multitude of his people embraced.

Christiana became a Saint, and her feast is kept on December 15th.

St. Gregory of Tours relates that when he was a boy his father fell gravely ill and lay dying. Gregory prayed fervently for his recovery. When Gregory was asleep at night, his Angel Guardian appeared to him and told him to **write the Name of Jesus** on a card and place this under the sick man's pillow.

In the morning Gregory acquainted his mother with the Angel's message, which she advised him to obey. He did so, and placed the card under his father's head, when, to the delight of the whole family, the patient grew rapidly better.

We could fill pages and pages with the miracles and wonders worked by the Holy Name at all times and in all places, not only by the Saints, but by all who invoke this Divine Name with reverence and faith.

Marchese says: "I refrain from relating here the miracles worked and graces granted by Our Lord to those who have been devoted to His Holy Name, because St. John Chrysostom reminds me that Jesus is always named when miracles are worked by holy men; hence, to attempt to enumerate them would be to try to give a list of the countless miracles which God has performed through all the ages, either to increase the glory of His Saints or to plant and strengthen the Faith in the hearts of men."

Cards of the Holy Name

Cards with the Holy Name inscribed on them have been used and recommended by the great lovers of the Holy Name, such as Msgr. André Dias (see page 9), St. Leonard of Port Maurice and St. Gregory of Tours, mentioned above.

Our readers would do well to use these cards, carrying them about on their persons during the day, putting them under their pillows at night and placing them on the doors of the rooms.

Chapter 7

The Saints and the
Holy Name

All the Saints had an immense love for and trust in the Name of Jesus. They saw in this name, as in a clear vision, all the love of Our Lord, all His Power, all the beautiful things He said and did when on earth.

They did all their wonderful works in the Name of Jesus. They worked miracles, cast out devils, cured the sick and gave comfort to everyone, using and recommending to all the habit of invoking the Holy Name. St. Peter and the Apostles converted the world with this all-powerful Name.

The Prince of the Apostles began his glorious career preaching the love of Jesus to the Jews in the streets, in the Temple, in their synagogues. His first striking miracle occurred on the first Pentecost Sunday when he was going into the Temple with St. John. A lame man, well known to the Jews, who frequented the Temple, stretched out his hand expecting to receive an alms. St. Peter said to him: "Silver and gold I have none; but what I have, I

19

give thee: In the name of Jesus Christ of Nazareth, arise, and walk." (*Acts* 3:6).

And instantly the lame man bounded to his feet and leaped for joy.

The Jews were astonished, but the great Apostle said to them: Why your wonder and surprise, as if we made this man sound by our own power? No, it is by the power of Jesus that this man walks.

Innumerable times since the days of the Apostle has the Name of Jesus been glorified.

We will quote a few of these countless examples, which show us how the Saints derived all their strength and consolation from **the Name of Jesus.**

St. Paul

St. Paul was in a very special way the preacher and doctor of the Holy Name. At first he was a fierce persecutor of the Church, moved by a false zeal and hatred for Christ. Our Lord appeared to him on the road to Damascus and converted him, making him the great Apostle of the Gentiles and giving him his glorious mission, which was to preach and make known His Holy Name to princes and kings, to Jews and Gentiles, to all nations and peoples.

St. Paul, filled with a burning love for Our Lord, began his great mission—uprooting paganism, casting down the false idols, confounding the philosophers of Greece and Rome, fearing no enemies and conquering all difficulties—**all in the Name of Jesus.**

St. Thomas Aquinas says of him: **"St. Paul** bore the Name of Jesus on his forehead because he gloried in proclaiming it to all men; he bore it on his lips because he loved to invoke it; on his hands, for he loved to write it in his epistles; in his heart, for his heart burned with love of it. He tells us himself: 'I live, yet not I, but Christ, liveth in me.'"

St. Paul tells us in his own beautiful way two great truths about the Name of Jesus.

First of all, he tells us of the infinite power of this Name. "In the Name of Jesus every knee shall bend in Heaven, on Earth and in Hell."

Every time we say, "Jesus," we give infinite joy to God, to all Heaven, to God's Blessed Mother and to the Angels and Saints.

Secondly, he tells us how to use it. "Whatever you do in word or in work, do all in the Name of Our Lord Jesus Christ." He adds: Whether you eat or whether you drink, or **whatever** else you do, do all in the Name of Jesus.

This advice all the Saints followed, so that their every act was done for love of Jesus, and therefore their every act and thought won them graces and merits. It was by this Name that they became Saints. If we follow this same advice of the Apostle, we too shall reach a very high degree of sanctity.

How are we to do everything in the Name of Jesus? By acquiring the habit, as we have said, of repeating the Name of Jesus frequently in the course of the day. This presents no difficulty—it only demands good will.

St. Augustine, the great Doctor of the Church, found his delight in repeating the Holy Name. He himself tells us that he found much pleasure in books which made frequent mention of this all-consoling Name.

St. Bernard felt a wonderful joy and consolation in repeating the Name of Jesus. He felt it, as he says, like honey in his mouth and a delicious peace in his heart. We too shall feel immense consolation and shall feel peace steal into our souls if we imitate St. Bernard and repeat frequently this Holy Name.

St. Dominic spent his days preaching and discussing with heretics. He always went on foot from place to place, as well in the oppressive heats of the summer as in the cold and rain of winter. The Albigensian heretics, whom he tried to convert, were more like demons let loose from Hell than mortal men. Their doctrine was infamous and their crimes enormous. Yet, as another St. Paul, he converted 100,000 of these wicked men, so that many of them became eminent for sanctity. Wearied at night with his labors, he asked only for one reward, which was to pass the night before the Blessed Sacrament, pouring out his soul in love for Jesus. When his poor body could resist no longer, he leaned his head against the altar and rested a little, after which he began once more his intimate converse with Jesus. In the morning, he celebrated Mass with the ardor of a seraph so that at times his body was raised in the air in an ecstasy of love. The Name of Jesus filled his soul with joy and delight.

Blessed Jordan of Saxony, who succeeded St. Dominic as Master General of the Order, was a preacher of great renown. His words went straight to the heart of his hearers, above all when he spoke to them of Jesus.

Learned professors of the university cities came with delight to hear him, and so many of them became Dominican friars that others feared to come, lest they too should be induced to join his Order. So many were drawn by Blessed Jordan's irresistible eloquence that, when his visit to a city was announced, the prior of the convent bought at once a great quantity of white cloth to make habits for those who were sure to seek entrance to the Order. Blessed Jordan himself received one thousand postulants to the habit, among whom were the most eminent professors of the European universities.

St. Francis of Assisi, that burning Seraph of love, found his delight in repeating the loved Name of Jesus. St. Bonaventure says that his face lit up with joy and his voice showed by its tender accents how much he loved to invoke this all-Holy Name.

No wonder, then, that he received on his hands and feet and side the marks of the five Wounds of Our Lord, a reward of his burning love.*

St. Ignatius of Loyola was second to none in his love for the Holy Name. He gave to his great Order not his own name, but rather he called it the "Society of Jesus." This divine Name has been, as it were, a shield and defense of the Order against its enemies and a guarantee of the holiness and sanctity of its members. Glorious, indeed is the great Society of Jesus.

St. Francis de Sales has no hesitation in saying that those who have the custom of repeating the Holy Name frequently may feel certain of dying a holy and happy death.

And indeed there can be no doubt of this, because every time we say, "Jesus," we apply the saving Blood of Jesus to our souls, while at the same time we implore God to do as He has promised, granting us everything we ask in His Name. All who

---

*Here we should also mention St. Bernardine of Siena (1380–1444), a Franciscan priest who was possibly the greatest propagator ever of devotion to the Holy Name of Jesus. St. Bernardine's fiery sermons attracted great crowds all over Italy as he preached devotion to the Holy Name. —*Editor*, 1993.

desire a holy death can secure it by repeating the Name of Jesus. Not only will this practice obtain for us a holy death, but it will lessen notably our time in Purgatory and may very possibly deliver us altogether from that dreadful fire.

Many Saints spent their last days repeating constantly, "Jesus, Jesus."

All the Doctors of the Church agree in telling us that the devil reserves his fiercest temptations for our last moments, and then he fills the mind of the dying person with doubts, fears and dreadful temptations—in the hope, at last, of carrying the unfortunate soul to Hell. Happy those who in life have made sure of acquiring the habit of calling on the Name of Jesus.

Facts like these we have just mentioned are to be found in the lives of all the great servants of God who became Saints and reached the highest degrees of sanctity by this simple and easy means.

St. Vincent Ferrer, one of the most famous preachers that the world has ever heard, converted the most abandoned criminals and transformed them into the most fervent Christians. He converted 80,000 Jews and 70,000 Moors, a prodigy we read of in the life of no other Saint. Three miracles are demanded by the Church for the canonization of a Saint; whereas in the bull of canonization of St. Vincent, 873 are mentioned.

This great Saint burned with love for the Name

of Jesus and with this Divine Name worked extraordinary wonders.

We, therefore, sinful as we are, can, with this Omnipotent Name, obtain every favor and every grace. The weakest mortals can become strong, the most afflicted find in it consolation and joy.

Who then can be so foolish or negligent as not to acquire the habit of repeating, "Jesus, Jesus, Jesus," constantly. It robs us of no time, presents no difficulty and is an infallible remedy for every evil.

Blessed Gonçalo of Amarante reached a very eminent degree of sanctity by the frequent repetition of the Holy Name.

Blessed Giles of Santarem felt so much love and delight in saying the Holy Name that he was raised in the air in ecstasy.

Those who repeat frequently the **Name of Jesus** feel a great peace in their soul, "that peace which the world cannot give," which God alone gives, a peace "that surpasses all understanding."

St. Leonard of Port Maurice cherished a tender devotion to the Name of Jesus and in his continual missions taught the people who thronged to listen to him the wonders of the Holy Name. This he did with such love that tears flowed from his eyes and from the eyes of all who heard him.

He begged them to put a card with this Divine

Name on their doors. This was attended with the happiest results, for many were thus saved from sickness and disasters of various kinds.

One, unfortunately, was prevented from doing so, since a Jew, who was part-owner of the house in which he lived, sternly refused to have the Name of Jesus placed on the door. His fellow-lodger then decided that he would write it on his windows, which he accordingly did. Some days after, a fierce fire broke out in the building, which destroyed all the apartments belonging to the Jew; whereas, the rooms belonging to his Christian neighbor in no wise suffered from the conflagration.

This fact was made public and increased a hundredfold faith and trust in the Holy Name of our Saviour. In fact, the whole city of Ferrajo was a witness of this extraordinary protection.

St. Edmund had special devotion to the Name of Jesus, which Our Lord Himself taught him.

One day when he was in the country and separated from his companions, a beautiful child stood by him and asked, "Edmund, do you not know me?" Edmund answered that he did not. Then replied the child, "Look at me and you will see who I am." Edmund looked as he was bidden and saw written on the Child's forehead, **"Jesus of Nazareth, King of the Jews."** "Know now who I am," said the Child. "Every night make the Sign of the Cross and say these words: 'Jesus of Nazareth, King of the Jews.'

If you do so, this prayer will deliver you and all who say it from sudden and unprovided-for deaths."

Edmund faithfully did as Our Lord told him. The devil once tried to prevent him and held his hands so that he could not make the holy sign. Edmund invoked the **Name of Jesus,** and the devil fled in terror, leaving him unmolested in the future.

Many people practice this easy devotion and so save themselves from unhappy deaths. Others, with their forefinger, imprint with holy water on their foreheads the four letters, "I.N.R.I.," to signify *Jesus Nazarenus, Rex Judaeorum*, the words written by Pilate for the Cross of Our Lord.

St. Alphonsus earnestly recommends both these devotions.

St. Frances of Rome enjoyed the extraordinary privilege of constantly seeing and speaking to her Angel Guardian. When she pronounced the Name of Jesus, the Angel was radiant with happiness and bent down in loving adoration.

Sometimes the devil dared to appear to her, seeking to frighten her and do her harm. But when she pronounced the Holy Name, he was filled with rage and hatred and fled in terror from her presence.

St. Jane Frances de Chantal, that most lovable friend of St. Francis de Sales, had many beautiful devotions taught her by this holy Doctor, who for many years acted as her spiritual adviser. She so loved the Name of Jesus that she actually wrote it with a hot iron on her breast. Blessed Henry Suso had done the same with a pointed steel rod.

We may not aspire to this holy daring; we may with reason lack the courage of inscribing the Holy Name on our breast. This needs a special inspiration from God. But we may follow the example of another dear Saint, viz., Blessed Catherine of Racconigi, a daughter of St. Dominic, who repeated frequently and lovingly the Name of Jesus, so that after her death, the Name of Jesus was found engraved in letters of gold on her heart. We all can do as she did, and thus the Name of Jesus will be emblazoned on our souls for all Eternity in the sight of the Saints and Angels in Heaven.

St. Gemma Galgani. Almost in our own day this dear girl Saint also had the privilege of frequent and intimate converse with her Angel Guardian. Sometimes the Angel and Gemma entered into a holy contest as to which of them could say more lovingly the Name of Jesus.

Her interviews with the dear Angel were of a simple and familiar nature. She chatted with him, gazed on his face, asked him many questions, to which he replied with ineffable love and affection.

He took messages from her to Our Lord, to the Blessed Virgin and the Saints and brought her back their answers.

Moreover, this glorious Angel took the tenderest

care of his protégée. He taught her to pray and meditate, especially on the Passion and sufferings of Our Lord. He gave her admirable counsels and lovingly reproved her when she committed any little faults. Under his guidance, Gemma speedily reached a high degree of perfection.

Chapter 8

The Doctrine of the Holy Name

We shall now explain the doctrine of the Holy Name—the most important chapter in this booklet—in order to show our readers whence comes the power and the divine value of this name and how the Saints worked their wonders by it and how we ourselves can obtain by its means every grace and blessing.

You may ask, Dear Reader, how it is that one word can work such prodigies?

I answer that with a word God made the world. With His word, He called out of nothing the sun, the moon, the stars, the high mountains and the vast oceans. By His word He sustains the whole universe in existence.

Does not the priest, too, in Holy Mass, work a prodigy of prodigies; does he not transform the little white host into the God of Heaven and earth by the words of Consecration; and though God alone can pardon sin, does not the priest also in the confessional pardon the blackest sins and the most awful crimes?

How? Because God gives to his words this infinite power.

So, too, God in His immense goodness gives to *each of us* an all-powerful word with which we can do wonders for Him, for ourselves and for the world. That word is **"Jesus."**

Remember what St. Paul tells us about it. That it is "a name above all names," and that . . .

"In the Name of Jesus, every knee shall bend in Heaven, on earth and in Hell."

But why?

Because **"Jesus"** signifies "God-made-man," viz., the Incarnation. When the Son of God became man, He was called "Jesus," so that when we say, **"Jesus,"** we offer to the Eternal Father the infinite love, the infinite merits of Jesus Christ; in a word, we offer Him His own Divine Son Himself; we offer Him the great Mystery of the Incarnation. Jesus IS the Incarnation!

How few Christians have any adequate idea of this sublime mystery, and yet it is the greatest proof that God has given, or could give us, of His personal love for us. *It* is everything to us.

The Incarnation

God became man for love of us, but what does it avail us if we do not understand this love?

God, the Infinite, Immense, Eternal, all-powerful God, the mighty Creator, the God that fills Heaven with His Majesty, hid all His power, His Majesty, His greatness, and became a little child in order to become like us and so to gain our love.

He entered into the pure womb of the Virgin Mary and there lay hidden for nine whole months. Then He was born in a stable between two animals. He was poor and humble. He passed 33 years working, suffering, praying, teaching His beautiful Religion, working miracles, doing good to all. He did all this to prove His love for *each* of us and so constrain us to love Him.

This stupendous act of love was so great that not even the highest Angels in Heaven could have conceived it possible, had not God revealed it to them.

It was so great that the Jews, God's chosen people, who were expecting a Saviour, were scandalized at the thought that God could humble Himself so much.

The Gentile philosophers, notwithstanding their vaunted wisdom, said that it was madness to think that the Almighty God could do so much for love of man.

St. Paul says that God exhausted all His power, wisdom and goodness in becoming man for us: "He emptied Himself out."

Our Lord confirms the words of the Apostle, for He says: "What more could I do?"

All this God did, not for all men in general, but for *each one* of us in particular. Think, think, of this.

Do you believe, do you understand, Dear Reader, that God loves you so much, that He loves you so intimately, so personally. What a joy, what a consolation if you really knew and felt that the great God loves you—*you*, so sincerely!

Our Lord has done still more, for He has made over to us all His infinite merits so that we can offer them to the Eternal Father as often as we like, a hundred, a thousand times a day.

And that is what we can do **each time** we say "**Jesus,**" if only we remember what we are saying.

You are perhaps surprised at this wonderful doctrine; you may never have heard it before?

But now at last that you know the infinite wonders of the Name of **Jesus**, say this Holy Name constantly; say it devoutly.

And in the future, when you say, "Jesus," remember that you are offering to God all the infinite love and merits of His Son. You are offering Him His own Divine Son. You cannot offer Him anything holier, anything better, anything more pleasing to Him, anything more meritorious for yourself.

How ungrateful are those Christians who never thank God for all He has done for them. Men and women live 30, 50, 70 years and never think of thanking God for all His wonderful love.

When you say the Name of Jesus, remember, too, to *thank* Our Sweet Lord for His Incarnation.

When He was on Earth, He cured ten lepers of their loathsome disease. They were delighted and went away full of joy and happiness, but only one came back to thank Him! Jesus was very hurt and said: "Where are the other nine?"

Has He not much more reason to feel grieved and hurt with you and me, who thank Him so little for all He has done for us in the Incarnation and in His Passion.

St. Gertrude was wont to thank God often, with a little ejaculation, for His goodness in becoming man for her. Our Lord appeared to her one day and said, "My dear Child, every time you honor My Incarnation with that little prayer, I turn to My Eternal Father and I offer all the merits of the Incarnation for you and for all those who do as you do."

Shall we not then try to say often, **"Jesus, Jesus, Jesus,"** sure of receiving a like wonderful grace.

The Passion

The second meaning of the word "Jesus" is "Jesus dying on the Cross," for St. Paul tells us that Our Lord merited this most Holy Name by His sufferings and death.

Therefore, when we say, "Jesus," we should also wish to offer the Passion and Death of Our Lord to the Eternal Father for His greater glory and for our own intentions.

Just as Our Lord became man for each one of us, as if each one of us were the only one in existence, so He died, not for all men in general, but for each one in particular. When He was hanging on the

Cross, He saw me, He saw you, Dear Reader, and offered every pang of His dreadful agony, every drop of His Precious Blood, all of His humiliations, all the insults and outrages He received, for *me*, for *you*, for *each one of us!* He has given us all these infinite merits as our very own. We may offer them hundreds and hundreds of times every day to the Eternal Father—for ourselves and for the world.

We do this *every* time we say "Jesus." At the same time, let us wish to *thank* Our Lord for all He has suffered for us.

It is appalling that many Christians know so little of this Holy Name and all that it means. As a result, they are losing precious graces every day, and they are forfeiting the greatest rewards in Heaven. Sad, deplorable ignorance!

How to Share in 500,000 Masses

The third intention we ought to have when saying "Jesus" is to offer all the Masses that are being said all over the world for the glory of God, for our own needs, and for the world at large. About 500,000 Masses are celebrated daily. And we can and should share in all of these.

The Mass brings Jesus to our altars. At every Mass He is once again present here on earth, as really as when He became man in His Mother's womb. He also sacrifices Himself on the Altar as really and truly as He did on Calvary, though in a mystical, unbloody manner. The Mass is said, not only for all those who assist at it in church, but for all those who wish to hear it and offer it with the priest.

All we have to do is to say reverently, **"Jesus, Jesus,"** with the intention of offering these Masses and participating in them. By doing this we have a share in all of them.

It is a wonderful grace to assist at and to offer one Mass; what will it not be to offer and share in 500,000 Masses every day!

Therefore, *every time* we say "Jesus," let it be our intention

1. To offer to God all the infinite love and merits of the Incarnation.

2. To offer to God the Passion and Death of Jesus Christ.

3. To offer to God all the 500,000 Masses being celebrated in the world— for His glory and our own intentions.

All that we have to do is to say the one word, "Jesus," but knowing what we are doing.

St. Mechtilde was accustomed to offer the Passion of Jesus in union with all the Masses of the world for the souls in Purgatory.

Our Lord once showed her Purgatory open and thousands of souls going up to Heaven as the result of her little prayer.

When we say, "Jesus," we can offer the Passion and the Masses of the world, either for ourselves or for the souls in Purgatory, or for any other intention we please.

We should *always*, too, offer them for the world at large and our own country in particular.

Chapter 9

We Can Ask for Everything
In the Name of Jesus

The Angels are our dearest and best friends and are most ready and able to help us in every difficulty and danger.

It is most regrettable that many Catholics do not know, love and ask the Angels for help. The easiest way to do so is **to say the Name of Jesus in their honor.** This gives them the greatest joy. They in return will help us in all our troubles and keep us safe from many dangers.

Let us say the Name of Jesus in honor of all the Angels, but especially in honor of our dear Angel Guardian, who loves us so much.

Our Sweet Lord is present in millions of consecrated Hosts in the countless Catholic churches of the world. During many hours of the busy day and during the long nights, He is forgotten and left alone.

We can do much to console and comfort Him by saying, "My Jesus, I love and adore Thee in all the Consecrated Hosts of the world, and I thank Thee with all my heart for remaining on all the altars of the world for love of us." Then say twenty, fifty or more times the Name of **Jesus** with this intention.

We may do most perfect penance for our sins by offering the Passion and Blood of Jesus many times each day for this intention.

The Precious Blood purifies our souls and raises us to a high degree of holiness. It is all so easy! We have only to repeat lovingly, joyfully, reverently, **"Jesus, Jesus, Jesus."**

If we are sad or cast down, if we are worried with fears and doubts, this Divine Name will give us a delightful peace. If we are weak and wavering, it will give us a new strength and energy. Did not Jesus, when on Earth, go about consoling and comforting all those who were unhappy? He is still doing it every day for those who ask Him.

If we are suffering from weak health, if we are in pain, if some disease is taking hold of our poor bodies, He can cure us. Did He not cure the sick, the lame, the blind, the lepers? Does He not say to us, "Come to Me, all you who labor, and are heavily burdened, and I will refresh you." Many could have good health if they only asked Jesus for it. By all means consult doctors, use remedies, but *above all* call on *Jesus!*

The Name of Jesus is the shortest, the easiest, the most powerful of all prayers. Our Lord tells us that anything we ask the Father in His Name, viz., in the Name of Jesus, we shall receive. Every time we say, "Jesus," we are saying a fervent prayer for all, all that we need.

The Souls in Purgatory. It is very lamentable that so many Christians forget and neglect the souls in Purgatory. It is possible that some of our dear friends are suffering in these dreadful fires, waiting, waiting for our prayers and help—which we could so easily give them and do not give them.

We have pity for the poor whom we see in the streets, for the hungry and for all those who suffer. None suffer so terribly as the souls in Purgatory, for the fire of Purgatory, as St. Thomas tells us, is the same as the fire of Hell!

How often, Dear Reader, do *you* pray for the Holy Souls? Days and weeks and perhaps months pass and you do little, perhaps nothing, for them!

You can easily help them if you will say frequently the Name of Jesus, because a) you thus offer for them the Precious Blood and suffering of Jesus Christ, as we have explained, b) you gain 300 days indulgence* every time you say **"Jesus."**

Having the custom of repeating often the Holy Name, you can, like St. Mechtilde, relieve thousands of souls, who will thereafter never cease praying for you with incredible fervor.

---

*See footnote on page 4. *—Editor*, 1993.

The Awful Crime of Ingratitude

We thank our friends most effusively for any little favor they do us, but we forget or neglect to thank God for His immense love of us, for becoming man for us, for dying for us, for all the Masses we can hear and the Holy Communions we can receive—and do not receive. What black ingratitude!

By repeating often the Name of Jesus, we correct this grave fault and thank God and give Him great joy and glory.

Do you not wish to give joy to God? You do? Then, Dear Friend, **thank, thank God!** He is waiting for your thanks.

God Loves Each One

We have said that Our Lord in the dreadful sufferings of His Passion, in the Agony in the Garden, when He was hanging on the Cross, saw us all and offered *for each one of us* every pang of pain, every drop of His Precious Blood.

Can it be possible that God is so good that He thinks of each one of us, that He loves each of us so much?

Our poor hearts and minds are small and mean and find it hard to believe that God can be so good, that He troubles Himself about us.

But God, as He is Omnipotent, as He is infinitely wise, is also *infinitely good and generous and lov-*

ing. To understand how God thought of each one of us during the Passion, when He was hanging on the Cross, we have only to remember what happens in the millions of Holy Communions received every day.

God comes to each one of us, with all the plenitude of the Divinity. He enters into each one as fully and entirely as He is in Heaven. He comes into each one of us as if that one person were the only one who received Him that day. **He comes with infinite, personal love!** That we all believe.

And how does He enter into us? He does not merely come into our mouths, our hearts—He comes into our souls, He unites Himself to our souls so intimately that He becomes in a marvelous way *one* with us.

Let us think for a moment of how the Great, Almighty, Eternal God is in our very soul in the most intimate possible way, that He is there with all His infinite love, that He remains there, not for a moment but for five, ten or more minutes—and this not once, but every day, if we so wish.

If we think about and understand this, it will be easy to see how He offered all His merits and all His sufferings for each one of us.

Chapter 10

The Devil and the Name of Jesus

The great, great evil, the great danger that threatens *each* of us *every* day and *every* night of our lives, is the *devil*.

St. Peter and St. Paul warn us in the strongest language to *beware* of the devil, for he is using all his tremendous power, his mighty intelligence to ruin us, to harm, to hurt us in every way. There is no danger, no enemy in the world we have to fear as we should fear the devil.

He cannot attack God, so he turns all his implacable hatred and malice against us.

We are destined to take the thrones he and the other bad angels have lost. This lashes him into wild fury against us. Many foolish, ignorant Catholics never think of this; they take no care to defend themselves and thus *allow* the devil to inflict on them infinite harm and cause them untold sufferings.

Our best, our easiest remedy is the Name of Jesus. It drives the devil flying from our sides and saves us from countless evils.

Oh, Dear Readers, say constantly this all-powerful

Name and the devil can do you no harm. Say it in all dangers, in all temptations. Wake up if you have been asleep. Open your eyes to the terrible enemy who is ever seeking your ruin.

Priests should preach frequently on this all-important subject, They should warn their penitents in the confessional against the devil. They counsel people to avoid bad companions, who make them lead bad lives. Incomparably more dreadful is the influence of the devil on them.

Teachers, catechists and mothers should constantly warn their children against the devil.

All their efforts will be only too little!

SAINT BENEDICT † PRESS

Saint Benedict Press, founded in 2006, is the parent company for a variety of imprints including TAN Books, Catholic Courses, Benedict Bibles, Benedict Books, and Labora Books. The company's name pays homage to the guiding influence of the Rule of Saint Benedict and the Benedictine monks of Belmont Abbey, North Carolina, just a short distance from the company's headquarters in Charlotte, NC.

Saint Benedict Press is now a multi-media company. Its mission is to publish and distribute products reflective of the Catholic intellectual tradition and to present these products in an attractive and accessible manner.

TAN · BOOKS

TAN Books was founded in 1967, in response to the rapid decline of faith and morals in society and the Church. Since its founding, TAN Books has been committed to the preservation and promotion of the spiritual, theological and liturgical traditions of the Catholic Church. In 2008, TAN Books was acquired by Saint Benedict Press. Since then, TAN has experienced positive growth and diversification while fulfilling its mission to a new generation of readers.

TAN Books publishes over 500 titles on Thomistic theology, traditional devotions, Church doctrine, history, lives of the saints, educational resources, and booklets.

For a free catalog from Saint Benedict Press
or TAN Books, visit us online at
saintbenedictpress.com • tanbooks.com
or call us toll-free at
(800) 437-5876